A WINE LOVER'S GUIDE TO NEW WORLD WINE

A Taste of Wine series

Harry Price

Kindle Direct Publishing

He causes the grass to grow for the cattle,
And vegetation for the labor of man,
So that he may bring forth food from the earth,
And wine which makes man's heart glad,
So that he may make his face glisten with oil,
And food which sustains man's heart.

PSALM 104:14-15

CONTENTS

EDITORIAL CREDIT

A Wine Lovers Guide to New World Wine

A Taste of Wine series

Edited by

Cup & Quill Editing and Publication Services

Rebecca Stohler: Associate Editor

Dr. Linda Tucker

ACKNOWLEDGMENTS

Much thanks to all those in the world of wine who have gone before and laid down solid ground for others to trod. I could not have written this book without these wonderful works: Karen MacNeil's *The Wine Bible*, Madeline Puckette and Justin Hammack's *The Essential Guide to Wine*, David Bird's *Understanding Wine Technology*, the Society of Wine Educators *CSW Study Guide*, and *The Oxford Companion to Wine*. I also would like to thank my mother, who taught me to smell everything, my father, who taught me to be quiet and think. I want to thank my children, who never stop teaching me things, and my wife for teaching me patience.

INTRODUCTION

This book's focus is to make useful information about the wine regions of North America, South America, Australia, New Zealand, and South Africa accessible. The scope is high-level, not exhaustive, and meant to illuminate essential details. It is a starting point for the exploration and enjoyment of non-European wine. Included are country and regional overviews, recommendations of signature wines, wine profiles, explanation of bottle label terms, classification of wine, and historical tidbits.

PREFACE

If it were not for an encounter long ago with a wine merchant's enthusiastic son in the Hudson Valley, I do not know where I would be with wine today. After observing me buying Mateus from the wine shop's cooler on several occasions, we started talking about his excursions to New York City as a wine buyer, his family's business, and drinking better wine. Later, we ended up talking about my taste preferences and walking the floor of his enormous wine store as he picked out bottle after bottle of wine with instructions to try them to see which I liked. I remember the wines, a Charles Krug Cabernet Sauvignon, a Côtes du Rhône Villages, and a Robert Mondavi blend. I had never known the exotic nature of wine, the intriguing aromas, and its suppleness. Wine was never the same; I was hooked. The young wine merchant spent his time helping, guiding, and introducing a stranger to good wine, and it is with the same spirit I wrote this book.

The path to publishing has not been easy or short, but certainly interesting. In 2019, after studying for a year, I passed the Certified Specialist of Wine (CSW) exam offered by the Society of Wine Educators. I immediately wanted to write a book but was advised not to, not yet. I was advised to first research, write, and publish articles, which I did for eighteen months on my website *www.worldofvino.com*, and still do. All the while, I was building up a small following on social media and studying for the next level of wine certification. I also experienced all the wine I reasonably could at social events, wine vacations, local wineries, private wine tastings, and home.

The time finally came for writing a book, and morning after morning, my ritual was the same month after month. I awoke before sunrise, fed the cat, researched, analyzed, and wrote for several hours a day. The result is in your hands, and it is my sincere hope you are helped, guided, informed, and inspired by this work.

FORMAT

The chapters and sections follow a standard format beginning with an introductory overview of each wine-producing country or region, location, place in the world of wine, broad climate features, and general perspective on winemaking. A description of wine regions follows this as it applies to the country or region. For each region, I included a historical tidbit of information; some are wine-related, some are not. This is followed by signature wine recommendations from prominent regions along with a taste profile of each. Experiencing the recommended wines will result in broad exposure to New World wine, its styles, and its grapes. You can branch out from that point, being guided by the additional information provided on regions of note. In most cases, only the notable regions are listed; with a few regions, the appellation list is exhaustive. If a region's wine is classified further, the details will be explained at the end of each section. The appendix contains a checklist of the recommended wines; this can be used to purchase wine and record your experiences.

APPROACHING WINE

Purchasing Wine

To improve your choices, use the information in this book to find wine from areas of the world you are interested in, along with available reviews and ratings. The popular 100-point rating system that appears on some wine labels was made famous by wine critic Robert Parker. Knowing an expert's ratings can help, keeping in mind that not all wine is rated, and there is no substitute for tasting for yourself.

The 100-point rating system considers the clarity, depth of color, aroma intensity, sweetness, acidity, bitterness, tannin, alcohol, body, flavors, complexity, and finish. The rating is relative to other wines of that type; for example, a 92-point California Chardonnay is a rating among Chardonnays from that region. Wine rating scores, from a major wine firm:

60-69 flawed and not recommended

70-79 flawed and taste average

80-84 above average to good

85-90 good to very good

90-94 superior to exceptional

95-100 benchmark examples or classic

Wine reviewing companies with online and subscription-based information are plentiful; three well-known entities are *Wine Spectator* (WS), *The Wine Advocate* (WA), and *Wine Enthusiast* (WE). You may see their ratings included with wine descriptions in wine stores.

Caring For Wine

In the short term, after purchasing wine, keep it cool and out of sunlight; for long-term cellaring, attempt to replicate the conditions of a cave. Keep the temperature stable and between 50-59 degrees Fahrenheit, the humidity at 60-75%, and eliminate light exposure.

Serving Wine

The usual alcohol range for wine is from 12% to 15% alcohol by volume (ABV), with 12% as the average. For comparison, beer is 5% ABV and, liquor is 40% ABV on average. Aerate red wine in a decanter, a bowl, or glasses at least fifteen minutes before serving, longer for complex wines. Aerating or allowing the wine to breathe mixes oxygen with the wine, improving its aroma and flavors. Just removing the cork alone will not expose the wine to enough oxygen.

Decant old wine leaving the sediment behind; it can be bitter and unsightly. Use good quality wine glasses with a thin rim to concentrate the aromas to your nose. Serve wine at a proper temperature to improve the aroma and flavor.

After opening a bottle, keep the temperature stable with ice for sparkling and sweet wine and a ceramic wine sleeve for all others. For maximum enjoyment, follow these serving temperature guidelines. Refrigerator temps are from 37-40 F, room temperature is 72 F; neither are optimal for serving wine.

High-end reds: 59-61 F

Reds, rosé, good whites: 50-54 F

Sweet wine, Champagne: 43-46 F

Tasting Wine

It is essential to know the components of wine and how they affect your tasting experience. Dry wines have no detectable sweetness. Off-dry or semi-sweet wines have a little sweetness, and sweet wines are noticeably sweet, while dessert wines are thick with sweetness.

Wine acidity will cause you to pucker as when eating a tart apple, tannins will dry your mouth, alcohol may cause your nose to burn somewhat, and bitterness is detected at the back of your tongue. After swallowing, look for a pleasant finish, a lingering taste; the longer, the better. Also, be on the lookout for odd tastes, bad tastes, unbalanced tastes, or if the wine's flavor does not linger at all, these are signs of wine flaws.

Wine Pairing With Food

Wine should complement or intensify food components; for example, acidic Chianti intensifies acidic tomato sauce, and a crisp acidic Chenin Blanc complements creamy cheese. The shared components of food and wine are sweetness, acidity, bitterness, savoriness, power, and intensity. Food also has salt and fat, strength of flavors, serving temps, and a preparation type. Try out parings before serving them to guests; there is no substitute for experimentation with food and wine pairing.

The Price Of Wine

I have been asked about the cost of wine, especially expensive wine. To start with the price of expensive wine is based on the earned reputation of a producer making great wine year over year. Also, there is not an endless amount of wine from the best vineyards, so the law of supply and demand dictates prices too. Marketing, hype, and people with too much money come into play also, driving prices skyward.

Costs For Any Winery

There are costs for any winery that muat be factored in when considering wine's prices. If a winery is endowed with land, they are at a great advantage, but for new wineries land is a major expense. The cost of tractors, harvesters, fermentation tanks and bottling equipment is not cheap.

Creating and maintaining a vineyard's fencing, irrigation, and ground cover is costly. Winery buildings, tasting rooms, chateaux, barns must be maintained. The cost of bottles, labels, boxes for shipping wine adds up. Labor and equipment costs for hospitality, planting, pruning, harvesting, winemaking, and bottling are expensive. Marketing, media, and advertising cost money.

Frequently Used Terms

Botrytis: referred to as noble rot, a fungus that concentrates a grape's juice; beneficial for sweet wine.

Traditional Method, Méthode Champenoise, Classic Method: first a primary fermentation and bottling, then a second fermentation in the bottle by adding grams of yeast and rock sugar; this makes the bubbles.

Signature grapes, wine: specialty of a region.

Single varietal: wine made from only one grape type.

Vintage: wine produced from a specific year's grapes.

Terroir: all aspects affecting wine; climate, location, soil, winemaking.

UNITED STATES

History

The United States (U.S.) ranks fourth globally for wine production after France, Italy, and Spain. The U.S. consumes more of its wine than exports, while North Americans' consumption of wine is steadily rising. The U.S. has at least one winery in every state, but the big five producing states are California, Washington, Oregon, New York, and Virginia. The U.S. produces small amounts of wine from indigenous grapes; however, all but small amounts are from European grape varieties or French-American hybrids.

American Viticultural Areas

American Viticultural Areas, commonly called AVAs, are established by petitioning the Alcohol and Tobacco Tax and Trade Bureau (TTB). It is a part of the U.S. Treasury and collects alcohol taxes, among other duties. AVAs have features similar enough to produce wine that reflects its uniqueness. AVAs can be any size, but the smaller the AVA, the more possibility exists for creating a distinct, unique, and representative wine. In practice, large AVAs contain smaller, more distinct AVAs within their boundaries; for example, the famous Napa Valley AVA includes sixteen sub-AVAs.

American Wine Labels

Helpful information is found on U.S. wine labels. Wine label content, including label art, is controlled by the government via the TTB. The law states that the following information must appear on a wine's label: *a brand name - wine type - alcohol content - bottle volume - health warning - sulfite content statement - producer's name/address*.

The back label's description is not regulated but falls under truth-in-labeling practices.

Brand Name

A brand is typically the producer, winery, vineyard, or a brand of wine. Brand wines are named for marketing appeal only, ex: "Petite Petit," from Michael David Winery, Lodi CA. It is helpful to know more about the brand, the owner, the winemaker, and their winemaking approach. See if they have a range of offerings, low to high quality, with different brand names for each tier. Are their wines rated highly by wine store staff, friends, or wine professionals? Are they an organic producer, an overpriced producer, or have they been in the news lately?

Wine Type

For a single varietal wine, one made from one grape type, the wine's grape variety and origin will appear on the label. Origin is a country, state, county, AVA, or vineyard.

When both grape variety and origin are listed, at least 75% of the grapes used are of that variety. And the entire 75% or more were grown in the place of origin; this applies to country, state, or county.

If the name of an AVA is listed (ex: Monticello AVA in Virginia), at least 85% of the grapes must have been grown within its boundaries.

However, if the AVAs boundaries match a county or state, only 75% of the grapes must be grown there. For blends, all the grapes are not listed, only the wine's origin.

If the term *Estate Bottled* is on a label, this means 100% of the wine is from grapes grown on land owned or controlled by the winery in an AVA.

The estate winery must crush, ferment, finish, age, and bottle the wine in a continuous process on their premises. The winery and the vineyard must be in the same viticultural area. If a specific vineyard is listed, 95% of the grapes must be grown within its boundaries.

Alcohol Content

The ABV of wine ranges from 5% to 16%, fortified wines even higher, but most are in the 12% to 14% range. The mouthfeel of wine improves with alcohol; higher levels will feel richer, plumper, smoother, and have more body. Also, high alcohol wine can have ripe fruit flavors since very ripe grapes contain more sugar. More sugar translates to more alcohol once fermented.

You may not find the alcohol content on some labels! Wine with less than 14% ABV is labeled with either its alcohol content or the terms *Table Wine* or *Light Wine.* For wines over 14% ABV the alcohol content must be expressly stated.

Volume Of The Bottle

The net contents of a wine container must be stated in metric units of measure. The standard everyday size is a 750 mL bottle containing about five 5 oz glasses. Wine must be bottled in 50, 100, 187, 375, 500, 750 mL bottles. Also available are 1L, 1.5 L, or 3L containers; anything over 3L is bottled in even liter quantities.

Government Health Warning

Wine can bring pleasure to your life, and it can also punish you. Learn to drink responsibly, please! This warning is a mandatory requirement for all alcoholic beverages for sale in the U.S.

Sulfite Statement

Sulfites occur naturally in wine, more in red than white, and helps stabilize and preserve it. Sulfites are also added to wine in tiny quantities during winemaking to reduce oxygen exposure, prevent bacteria from growing, and unwanted yeast from fermenting prematurely.

A sulfite statement appears on labels for wines with more than ten parts per million of sulfur dioxide. Wine labeled as *organic* must be free of any artificially added sulfites. Those labeled as *made with organically grown grapes* will have some sulfites.

The Name And Address Of The Bottler Or Producer

Domestic wines may have this statement further qualified with terms such as *Produced*, meaning 75% or more of the wine was fermented at the stated address.

Vinted, which means that the wine was subjected to cellar treatment at the indicated address.

Produced and Bottled by is used when the wine was bottled at the winery where it was made.

CALIFORNIA

Fueled by the Gold Rush of 1849, hundreds of thousands of people moved to California. Soon after, wineries started to spring up in the late 1850s. Some of the wineries from this era still exist, to name a few, Charles Krug, and Inglenook wineries in Napa Valley, Gundlach Bundschu, and Buena Vista Wineries of Sonoma county. Immigrant families from Italy, Hungary, France, Germany, Finland, and more contributed to early wine-making's growth and success.

California's Mediterranean-like climate provides a tremendous advantage for winegrowing. Dry, cool air descends from the north, down the coast, along river valleys, bays, and gaps in the coastal mountain ranges. Grapes thrive in the morning fog, hot, dry daytime, and cool nights in the inland mountains, hills, and valleys. Significant temperature swings from day to night make for ripe yet acidic fruit; both are essential components of good wine. The dry conditions also keep grapes healthy, making it difficult for fungus and molds to propagate.

There are five exceptionally large AVAs in California stretching for hundreds of miles from Mendocino County, located north of San Francisco, to Santa Barbara County in the south. They are The *North Coast, Sierra Foothills, San Francisco Bay, Central Coast* and *South Coast* AVAs. FYI, many AVAs exist outside of the big five.

These AVAs contain smaller, more distinct AVAs. For example, the North Coast AVA includes the Napa Valley and Sonoma County. Wine labeled with one of the big five AVAs may be good wine, but it is regional wine made from grapes grown anywhere within its large boundaries and will not represent specific terroir.

NORTH COAST AVA

North of San Francisco within the large North Coast AVA are the well-known wine regions of Napa Valley, Sonoma, and the lesser-known Mendocino AVA.

Napa Valley AVA

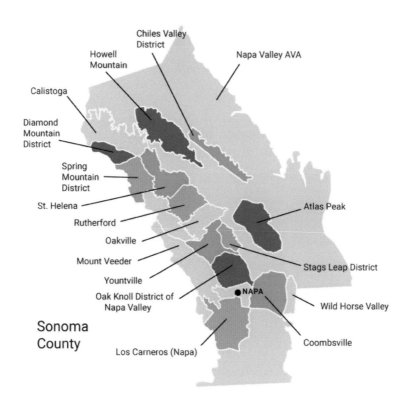

Think of American wine, and immediately Napa Valley comes to mind. The Napa Valley AVA is extensive, covering most of Napa County's 748 square miles. To its west is the Sonoma wine region and the Pacific Ocean. Nestled between the Vaca and Mayacamas mountains, vineyards line the hills along the thirty-mile-long valley.

The Napa River runs the valley's length, beginning high in the Mayacamas Mountains to the north. The northern end of the valley is narrow near Calistoga and widens near the cooler San Pablo Bay in the south. Napa produces world-class wines and uses oak aging for most of its wine. The long, hot, dry growing seasons are perfect for the late-ripening red Cabernet Sauvignon grapes that go into Napa Valley's signature wines.

Historical Tidbit

The sixty-acre Cole Ranch AVA is the smallest in the United States and lies within the North Coast AVA in Mendocino County.

Napa Valley Sub-AVAs

The Napa Valley AVA is not just one entity but comprises sixteen sub-AVAs with individual wine personalities. The sub-AVAs are understood from three terroir perspectives, valley floor AVAs, high elevation AVAs, and cooler south Napa Valley AVAs. The AVA's name will appear on wine labels along with the term *Napa Valley*. In many cases, the word *AVA* will not appear on labels.

Napa Valley Floor AVAs: these seven AVAs are known for world-class Cabernet Sauvignon wines made by some of the most famous wineries in the U.S. Listed from north to south are *Calistoga, St. Helena, Rutherford, Oakville, Yountville, Stags Leap,* and *Chiles Valley District*. These wines have all the right components, fruit, acid, body, tannin, and alcohol in all the correct proportions.

Napa Valley High Elevation AVAs: the five high-elevation AVA's vineyards sit above the valley floor, some on terraced mountainsides above the fog line between 400 and 2,600 feet. Due to the mountain terrain and temperature swings from day to night, the Cabernet Sauvignon and Zinfandel wine here is rich, lean, and ages well. Three AVAs located on the west side of the Napa Valley in the Mayacamas Mountains, listed from north to south, are the *Diamond Mountain District, Spring Mountain District,* and the *Mount Veeder AVA.* To the east of the Napa Valley, in the Vaca Mountains, are the *Howell Mountain* and the *Atlas Peak AVA*s.

South Napa Valley AVAs: the southern end of the Napa Valley is cooler due to the San Pablo Bay moderating the weather. These AVAs are known for excellent Chardonnay and Pinot Noir. They include *the Oak Knoll District of Napa Valley, Carneros,* the *Wild Horse Valley and Coombsville AVAs.*

Recommended Signature Wine

Any wine from one of Napa Valley's famous sub-AVAs is a winning choice. A recommended starting point is a Cabernet Sauvignon from the *Calistoga AVA*, the warmest in the Napa Valley. Expect deep red to purple wine with aromas of cassis, spice, citrus, browned toast, and high alcohol. Dark rich black fruit like blackberries and black cherries nicely dominate the flavor profile. All this is supported by a full-body, medium acidity, and pleasing tannins with lingering finishes.

Try a Chardonnay from the *Los Carneros AVA*, one of southern Napa Valley's cooler areas. These are beautiful light golden-colored wines, elegantly aged in oak, which contributes to toast, baked goods, and vanilla aromas. Expect ripe fruit flavors of apples and pineapple with a balance of all the necessary fruit, acid, and alcohol components, a full-body, and lingering finish.

Sonoma Appellations

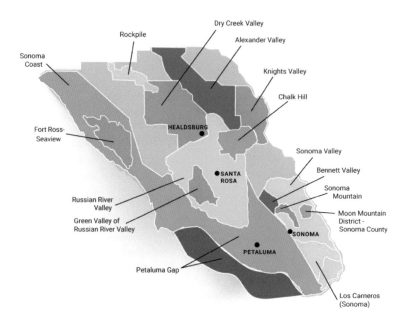

The Sonoma County wine region is much larger than its Napa Valley neighbor and has more diverse terrain. It has eighteen AVAs and sub-AVAs that produce world-class wines. Sonoma County sits on the Pacific Ocean, and the type of grapes grown in the coastal areas reflect the cool climate. Inland, coastal mountains protect Sonoma's vineyards, raise temperatures, reduce cold and precipitation, and allow for grapes such as Zinfandel to be crafted into outstanding wines.

Historical Tidbit

Fort Ross State Historic Park in Sonoma County was created in 1909 to preserve and study the outposts used from 1812-1842 by Russian fur traders.

Notable AVAs

Northern Sonoma AVA is a regional AVA covering most of Sonoma County. Wine with this designation on the label comes from grapes grown anywhere in the AVA.

Sonoma Coast AVA this AVA has two sub-AVAs, *Petaluma Gap* and *Fort-Ross Seaview AVAs*, and runs the entire Pacific coast of Sonoma County. Sub-AVA Fort-Ross Seaview is an 1800-foot-high-elevation wine area. These AVAs are known for wine made from cold tolerant Chardonnay, Pinot Noir, and Syrah grapes.

Russian River AVA and sub-AVAs have cool, foggy climates producing wine from Pinot Noir and Chardonnay grapes. Sub-AVA *Chalk Hill* produces notable Sauvignon Blanc.

Sonoma Valley AVA has a cool climate due to the San Pablo Bay's chilly air flowing up the Sonoma Creek valley. This area and its sub-AVAs, such as the *Sonoma Mountain AVA*, are known for Chardonnay, Pinot Noir, and sparkling wine. Sub-AVA *Los Carneros AVA,* close to the San Pablo Bay, makes exceptional sparkling wine, Chardonnay, and Pinot Noir.

Dry Creek Valley AVA and the high-elevation *Rock Pile AVA* are warmer than the coastal regions of Sonoma. They are known for delicious wine made from the Zinfandel grape.

Alexander Valley AVA runs along the Russian River's north-south before it turns west to the Pacific Ocean. This area is warm and produces big, juicy wines from Cabernet Sauvignon grapes.

Recommended Signature Wine

This area's recommendation is a Chardonnay from the *Chalk Hill AVA* in the Russian River Valley. These Chardonnays exhibit aromas of orange blossoms, crisp apples, pears, citrus, vanilla, and toasted spice with a creamy mouth-filling body. They are balanced wines with medium acidity and a good finish.

Try a red Zinfandel from the *Dry Creek Valley AVA* or the *Rock Pile AVA*. These are a delicious expression of the Zinfandel grape and excellent wines from the North Coast region. Expect very red wine, with aromas of jam, blackberries, blueberry, plums, caramel, and spice. Zinfandel has medium tannins, low acidity, and can be high in alcohol.

You must try a wine from the *Alexander Valley AVA*. These are big, juicy wines from Cabernet Sauvignon grapes, and you can expect complexity, power, black fruit flavors, and aromas of dried herbs, pipe tobacco, spice, along with nice acidity. These are elegant, dark-colored, age-worthy, and balanced wines

SAN FRANCISCO BAY AVA

This AVA is in a prime tourism location being close to San Francisco. Its challenge is to remain true to its roots and resist the urban sprawl of Silicon Valley. The two most prominent sub-AVAs producing excellent wines are the *Livermore Valley* and *Santa Clara Valley AVAs*.

Historical Tidbit

A registered California landmark, Wente Vineyards, started in 1883 in Livermore, California. It is the oldest continuously operating, family-owned winery in the United States.

Notable AVAs

Livermore Valley AVA produces unique white Bordeaux blends from Sémillon and Sauvignon Blanc grapes. With a Mediterranean climate, good gravelly vineyards, and cooling effect of the Bay, the area produces fine wine from Cabernet Sauvignon, Chardonnay, Merlot, Sangiovese, and Rhône varieties, such as Grenache.

Santa Clara Valley AVA is warm compared to San Francisco, with its vineyards sheltered by the foothills of the Santa Cruz Mountains. The area is considered a Mediterranean climate featuring great wine from old Zinfandel vineyards while also making good use of French varieties such as Cabernet Sauvignon, Merlot, Chardonnay, and Italy's Sangiovese grape.

Recommended Signature Wines

Try a Chardonnay from the *Livermore Valley AVA*. These are lush, ripe wines, with balance, pleasant aromas, and medium-bodied. Streaks of acidity help the mouthfeel and support refreshing pear, cream, and baking spice flavors.

This area's recommendation for a red wine is made with Zinfandel grapes from the *Santa Clara AVA*. These are deep red, fruit-filled wines with flavors of raspberries and blueberries, nice balance between acid and tannin.

Try a Cinsault from the Lodi AVA, Bechthold Vineyards. It has the oldest Cinsault vines in the world, planted in 1886. Technically the *Lodi AVA* is outside of the SF Bay AVA, but notable.

SIERRA FOOTHILLS AVA

Heading east across the vast Central Valley from the Napa Valley sits the *Sierra Foothills AVA*, located in the Sierra mountain's foothills. It has notable sub-AVAs producing wine from high elevation vineyards.

Historical Tidbit

The Gold Rush of 1848 began in El Dorado County when James Marshall discovered gold at Sutter's Mill, on the South Fork of the American River.

Notable AVAs

El Dorado AVA employs many European grape types, including French Syrah, Italian Barbera, German Gewurztraminer, to name a few. The region takes advantage of the breezes off the Sierra mountains that remove hot air from the vines and sweep down through the valley.

Fiddletown and California Shenandoah Valley AVAs: good wine from its most planted grape type, Zinfandel.

Recommended Signature Wines

This area's recommendation is a blend made with Syrah and Mourvèdre grapes from the *El Dorado AVA*. These are full of the aroma of violets, plums, cinnamon, and dried currant, followed by flavors of dark stone fruit, ripe cherries, black and white pepper shining through. The acidity and alcohol are on the high side but balanced, with a full, silky body and a dry finish.

CENTRAL COAST AVA

South of San Francisco within the vast *Central Coast AVA* are two general climate zones: the cooler coastal regions and the inland areas east of the coastal mountains. Covered here from north to south are *Monterey, Paso Robles, Santa Maria Valley, and Santa Ynez Valley AVAs.*

Notable AVAs

Monterey AVA is a long, reasonably narrow AVA with six sub-AVAs. The Monterey AVA is oriented north to the southeast, where the Salinas River runs between the Gabilan and Sierra de Salinas mountains paralleling the coast. Cooler air and resulting fog from the Monterey Bay flow southward, creating excellent growing conditions for grapes that grow well in cooler climates. In the *Santa Lucia Highlands, Arroyo Seco,* and the *Chalone AVAs* Chardonnay and Riesling grapes are prominent, with Chardonnay taking the production lead and Pinot Noir as the principal red grape.

The Monterey AVA's warmer southeast end is best for grapes needing heat and longer growing seasons. *San Lucas, Hames Valley,* and *San Bernabe AVA* sub-AVAs are perfect areas for Cabernet Sauvignon, Merlot, Malbec, Grenache, and Zinfandel grapes.

Paso Robles AVA this is a large, diverse AVA in San Luis Obispo County with eleven sub-AVAs known for producing beautiful Zinfandels and uses Bordeaux type grapes, Cabernet Franc, Malbec, and Merlot.

Santa Maria Valley AVA south of Paso Robles in Santa Barbara County is a cool weather region specializing in cool climate styles using Pinot Noir, Syrah, Chardonnay, and Pinot blanc grapes.

Santa Ynez Valley AVA has the largest concentration of vineyards in Santa

Barbara County. The AVA runs along the east-west valley of the Santa Ynez River. Vineyards in the western Pacific Ocean end of the valley are suited to the cooler-climate varieties of Pinot Noir, Chardonnay, and dessert wines helped by Botrytis cinerea (aka noble rot). The ocean's cooling influences taper off to the east, moving down through the valley. Therefore, the eastern end has more plantings of Cabernet Sauvignon, Merlot, Sauvignon Blanc, and Syrah.

Recommended Signature Wine

This area's recommendation is a wine made with Chardonnay grapes from the northern *Monterey AVA*. These Chardonnays are like French Chablis with light color and aromas of minerals, citrus, pepper, pear, crushed rock, and oyster shells. They have brilliant acidity, are lighter-bodied, balanced, and finish with long spiciness.

Try a red wine made from the Zinfandel grape from the *Paso Robles AVA*. They present deeply colored wines, with jammy red and black fruit, with coffee-like spices, medium-bodied, low acidity, and tannins that do not overpower.

SOUTH COAST AVA

South of the Central Coast AVA down the California coast south of Los Angeles lies the South Coast AVA. While this area is now residential and commercially developed and not known for wine production, the first vineyards in California were planted here by Franciscan missionaries in the late 1700s.

Today the South Coast's sub-AVAs are having good success with many grape types. To name a few, old vine Zinfandel, Petite Sirah, Cab Franc and Rhône varieties such as Viognier and Grenache. Spanish Tempranillo, and Italian Sangiovese fare well in the warm, misty climate too.

Notable AVAs

Temecula Valley AVA produces notable wines from Tempranillo, Sangiovese, Syrah, Cabernet Franc grapes at very reasonable prices.

Recommended Signature Wine

This area's recommendation is a wine made with Cabernet Franc grapes from the *Temecula Valley AVA.* Expect an elegant, aromatic wine full of complex flavors of red fruit, strawberry jam, and raspberry sauce.

WASHINGTON STATE

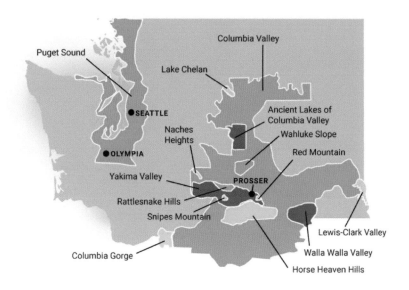

Behind California, the second-largest amount of vineyard acreage and wine production in the U.S. is in Washington State. Located in the northwest corner of the U.S., it borders Canada to the north, Oregon to the south, Idaho to the east, and the Pacific Ocean to the west. Wine production occurs on the dry eastern side of the Cascade Mountains along the Columbia, Yakima, and the Snake Rivers. Long days of sunshine, dry air, irrigation from mountain snow runoff, and high vineyard elevations create excellent wine production conditions. The Columbia Valley AVA is enormous; it contains eleven sub-AVAs. Wine labeled with this AVA is regional wine where grapes are sourced from anywhere in the AVA. Washington State has signature wine made from Riesling, Syrah, Chardonnay, and Cabernet Sauvignon grapes and uses oak barrels to age in many wines.

Historical Tidbit

In 2002, Quilceda Creek Winery was awarded a rare 100-point rating from wine critic Robert Parker for its old-vine Cabernet Sauvignon from Horse Heaven Hills and the Red Mountain AVAs.

Notable AVAs

Horse Heaven Hills AVA sits between the Yakima and Columbia rivers near Oregon's border. It has warm south-facing vineyards that produce Chardonnay, Syrah, and some of the best Cabernet Sauvignon wines in the U.S.

Walla Walla Valley AVA straddles Washington and Oregon's state line and sits in the sunny, dry Walla Walla River basin. It is known for producing lovely Syrah, Merlot, and Cabernet Sauvignon, with intense, rich flavors. The Chardonnay and Gewurztraminer grapes are used for their signature white wines.

Yakima Valley AVA has the most vineyards in the state and is known for great Chardonnay. Three sub-AVAs, The *Red Mountain, Snipes Mountain,* and *Rattlesnake Hills AVA*, reside within the Yakima Valley AVA.

Recommended Signature Wine

A good recommendation to start with is a Cabernet Sauvignon from *the Horse Heaven Hills AVA*. These are rich, pure, full-bodied wines with notes of blackberry, blueberries, cassis, spice, and chocolate. The tannins are layered, acidity medium, with a lingering finish.

Try a wine from the *Walla Walla Valley AVA* made from Syrah grapes. These are like Syrah from Australia or The Rhône Valley in France, with medium body, savory flavors of game, earth, leather, chocolate powder, and floral notes. The acidity and alcohol are on the high side but tamed and balanced.

OREGON

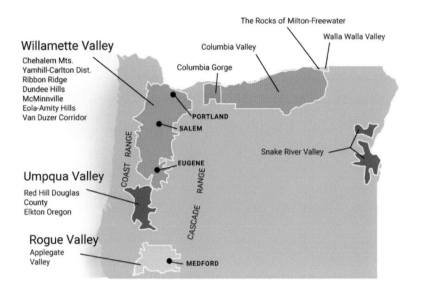

This state ranks third in wine production in the U.S., behind its southern neighbor California and northern neighbor Washington State. Oregon shares some AVAs with Washington and Idaho, but the Willamette Valley AVA and its sub-AVAs produce most of Oregon's wine. Oregon is a cool climate wine region, and its signature wines, Pinot Noir and Pinot Gris reflect this. Oregon uses American and French oak to age its wines.

Historical Tidbit

Astoria, Oregon, at the mouth of the Columbia River, was the first permanent English-speaking settlement west of the Rocky Mountains.

Notable AVAs

Willamette Valley AVA runs along the Willamette River Valley to the east of the coastal mountains. The area is cool, rainy, and like Burgundy, France where Pinot Noir reigns supreme. This AVA contains seven sub-AVAs that produce world-class Pinot Noir. For example, *Dundee Hills AVA,* noted for its Pinot Noir, has several wineries recognized worldwide.

Umpqua Valley and Rogue Valley AVAs are the warmer southern vineyards of Oregon perfectly suited for Cabernet Sauvignon and Merlot.

Snake River AVA is a high elevation viticultural region on the far eastern side of Oregon. It is suitable for Bordeaux-type grapes of Cabernet Franc, Cabernet Sauvignon, Malbec, and Merlot with good day to night temperature shifts. Chardonnay, Riesling, and Gewürztraminer grow well here, and the climate is cold enough to produce ice wine.

Columbia Valley AVA is shared with its northern neighbor Washington State and produces good Cabernet Sauvignon, Syrah, and Merlot.

Recommended Signature Wine

Start with a Pinot Noir from the *Willamette Valley AVA*. These are medium-bodied wines with low tannins and moderate acidity; oak-aged in French barrels, which brings subtle toasty notes. These lead with flavors and aromas of Mediterranean herbs, baker's chocolate, blueberries, cherries, raspberries, and spice.

NEW YORK

Most of New York state has a cold and snowy climate, much like Germany and Austria's wine regions. The cold winters, long springs, and short warm summers present challenges for winegrowing. Still, through persistence and proper grape selection, its AVAs produce signature wine with cold hearty grapes such as Cabernet Franc, Chardonnay, and Riesling. French-American hybrid grapes have been successful in New York along with indigenous grapes. The Cayuga grape, a French-American hybrid, was bred at nearby Cornell University specifically for the Finger Lakes climate.

Historical Tidbit

A commercial winery now exists in New York City. In the Williamsburg neighborhood of Brooklyn, excellent small-batch wines are made from grapes sourced from around the U.S.

Notable AVAs

Finger Lakes AVA is centered around the beautiful glacial Finger Lakes region in west-central New York and produces lovely wine. Its three sub-AVAs, *Cayuga Lake, Seneca Lake, Keuka Lake*'s vineyards, lie along the banks of the long, slender, and deep lakes. The largest of the lakes is Cayuga, at just under forty miles long and more than three miles wide. Award-winning ageable Rieslings are at the pinnacle of the region's success, but their wine from Chardonnay and Cabernet Franc grapes are unique and delicious.

Long Island AVA has two sub-AVAs, *Hamptons* and *the North Fork of Long Island AVAs*, producing wine two hours from New York City. The better growing conditions exist in the North Fork of Long Island AVA, an official maritime climate moderated by the Long Island Sound. The Bordeaux blends and single varietal wines made with French grape types Merlot, Cabernet Franc, Chardonnay, Riesling, and Sauvignon Blanc grapes are quite good.

Recommended Signature Wine

Start with a Cabernet Franc from the *Seneca Lake AVA*. These are medium red to black cherry-colored with medium body, fine tannin structure, clear focused, light, crisp, and brimming with aromas of lively cherries, touches of earthiness, and a little spice.

A Riesling is a must-try Finger Lakes wine from the *Keuka Lake AVA*. There are so many styles: semi-sweet, dry, reserve, late harvest. The issue is where to start. The recommended wine, to begin with, is a dry Riesling, one without any detectable sweetness. These are fragrant wines with spring fruit blossom scents, balanced acidity, crisp, refreshing, good mouthfeel, and a lingering finish.

VIRGINIA

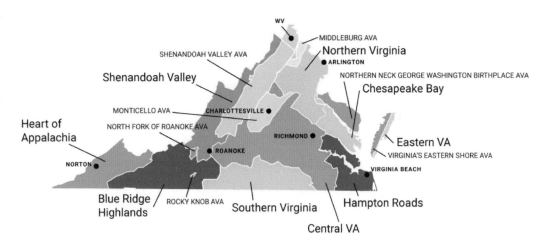

Virginia ranks fifth in wine production in the U.S., with seven AVAs (soon to be eight) producing delicious wine from French grapes, French-American hybrids, and the indigenous Norton grape. Most of Virginia's climate is of the humid subtropical classification due to the warm, moist air of the Gulf Stream blanketing the region. As you can see from the map Virginia has varying terrain and climate zones from maritime sandy beaches in the east to a central Coastal Plain to rolling hills tucked up against the Blue Ridge Mountains, where most of the vineyards exist.

East coast winegrowers face more difficult vineyard conditions than in California, with high summer humidity that fosters mold and disease followed by cold winters that can harm vines. Regardless, with careful planning and investigation, growers have found soil, sun, and a climate suitable for producing beautiful wines.

Expect neither a French nor California style wine from Virginia; it has its own style; not as fruity as California wines and not as earthy and minerally as French wines. Virginia red wines are deep-colored, restrained, and savory with medium acidity and smooth tannins. Aromas of raspberry, red currant, blueberry pie filling, herbs, and wet rock shine through.

Popular with winemakers are white Chardonnay, Petit Manseng, Sauvignon Blanc, and Viognier grapes. Red grapes that grow well in Virginia are Merlot, Cabernet Franc, Chambourcin, Grenache, Petit Verdot, Tannat, and the ever-present Cabernet Sauvignon. Virginia uses oak aging in many of its wines.

No one could have predicted that Viognier, an almost extinct and forgotten Northern Rhône grape, would find fame in the U.S., but here we are. Since its first plantings in Virginia by Horton Vineyards of Orange County in 1989, it has earned acclaim. In 2011 the Virginia Wine Board named Viognier Virginia's signature white grape.

Historical Tidbit

In Charlottesville, Virginia, Jefferson Vineyards within the Monticello AVA produces award-winning wine on a portion of Thomas Jefferson's Monticello estate.

Notable AVAs

Middleburg AVA is in the northern part of the Blue Ridge Mountain foothills with the Potomac River as its northern border. Wine tourism flourishes in this area due to the dense population of Washington D.C. and surrounding suburbs east of the vineyards. Many award-winning producers create award-winning single varietal wine from Cabernet Franc, Viognier, Albarino, Merlot, Petit Manseng, and Petit Verdot. Meritage blends produced as flagship wines are made by many wineries using the Bordeaux grapes Cabernet Sauvignon, Merlot, Cabernet Franc, Malbec, and Petit Verdot.

Monticello AVA is in the Blue Ridge Mountain eastern foothills, where vineyards are situated south-facing at high altitudes for maximum sun exposure. The Monticello AVA is a beautiful place that produces wine with depth of flavor and character due to excellent vineyard sites, the wineries' high expertise, and mature vineyards. The prominent grapes of this area are Cabernet Franc, Chardonnay, and Viognier.

Shenandoah Valley AVA is west the Blue Ridge Mountains and therefore shielded from the hot moist air typical east of the Blue Ridge. These conditions are very favorable for producing excellent wine grapes as is reflecting in award winning wines.

Recommended Signature Wines

Try a white wine made from Viognier grapes from the *Monticello AVA* near Charlottesville, Virginia. Viognier is known as the white wine for red wine lovers, and is light golden with a nice oily mouthfeel, low acidity, complex floral aromas, hints of anise, apricots, and peaches.

Another recommendation for a Virginia white wine is made from Petit Manseng grapes from the *Middleburg AVA* in Northern Virginia, near the charming town of Middleburg. Winemakers in Virginia create dry versions with no detectable sweetness. Petit Manseng is a lovely medium body wine with aromas of rich candied pineapple, sweet spice, wild honey, crushed cashew nuts, and creamy orange peel. It has low acidity and will improve with time in the cellar.

For a red recommendation, an excellent place to start is a Meritage from the *Monticello AVA*. These wines use Bordeaux grapes in varying proportions with Merlot or Cabernet Sauvignon as the leading grape blended with smaller amounts of Cabernet Franc, Malbec, and Petit Verdot.

Try an authentic North American wine made from the indigenous Norton grape. The most extensive vineyard of Norton grapes in Virginia is in the *Middleburg AVA* at Chrysalis Vineyards. Norton is deep purple-colored, rich, with dark fruit, fresh ripe plum, and tart red cherries flavors. These wines have good acidity, tannins and will improve with age.

CANADA

Ontario is the central high-quality winegrowing region in eastern Canada. The area specializes in ice-wine production and uses cold hearty Cabernet Franc, Chardonnay, and Riesling grapes. Ontario's winemaking occurs in the Niagara Peninsula's sub-regions on the southern shore of Lake Ontario, where the warming lake-effect moderates the climate. Wines that meet the quality control and appellation standards of the Vintners Quality Alliance (VQA) get labeled as *VQA* wine.

In western Canada's British Columbia, the highest quality designator is called *BC VQA;* the second is *Wines of Distinction.* The lowest quality bulk wines are without a quality indicator on labels and can use non-Canadian grapes. British Columbia's best wine region is east of the Pacific coastal mountains, where cool, dry conditions are favorable for cold hearty grapes.

Historical Tidbit

The first commercial winery in Canada opened its doors on the small Pelee Island in Lake Erie in Ontario, Canada, in 1866.

Notable Appellations

Beamsville Bench appellation is a sub-appellation in the western-most part of the Niagara Peninsula winegrowing region. The area produces fresh, elegant fruit-driven wines from Chardonnay, Riesling, and Pinot Noir grapes.

Okanagan Valley appellation produces a significant part of British Columbian wine along the Okanagan lakes. The cool, dry conditions are favorable for cold hearty Merlot, Pinot Gris, Chardonnay, and Pinot Noir.

Recommended Signature Wine

Try an ice-wine from *Niagara Peninsula appellation*. These are intense wines with concentrated grape sugars, but with balanced acidity and a surprisingly dry finish. Delicate tropical and citrus fruit flavors of peach, lemon, and mango shine through the sweetness. Ice-wine comes in many styles, including oak-aged, unoaked, and sparkling.

A red Pinot Noir from the *Okanagan Valley of British Columbia appellation* in the west of Canada is an excellent place to start. These are red, earthy-colored wines with aromas of fresh flowers, roses, cedar, and cherries. Their wines have tight acidity, structure, and flavors of red fruits such as cherries, cranberries, strawberries, warm spices, white pepper, and long finishes.

MEXICO

Mexico's wine industry is located primarily in the state of Baja California, Mexico, on the Pacific coast. The climate is Mediterranean-like; hot, dry, with low humidity and beneficial cool air coming off the Pacific Ocean. This region accounts for all but a small portion of Mexico's premium wine.

Mexico's government does not regulate any part of the wine industry, including labeling. The grapes used by winegrowers are French Bordeaux, Italian, and Spanish in origin, including well-known red varieties such as Cabernet Sauvignon, Cabernet Franc, Merlot, Malbec, Syrah, Pinot Noir, Zinfandel, Tempranillo, and Nebbiolo. The primary white grapes are Chardonnay, Chenin Blanc, Riesling, Sauvignon Blanc, and Viognier.

Historical Tidbit

Casa Madero is the oldest winery in the Americas. It was founded in August of 1597 as the San Lorenzo hacienda. It was given to Don Lorenzo Garcia by Philip II the king of Spain.

Notable Appellations

Valle de Guadalupe is the Mexican center for premium wine production located in the state of Baja California, Mexico.

Recommended Signature Wine

A red Nebbiolo from the *Valle de Guadalupe* is an excellent place to start. These are ruby-colored wines with aromas of ripe red fruit, spice, leather, and tobacco. Nebbiolo is a tannic wine with good acidity, and the better ones will soften and improve with age.

WINE FESTIVALS USA-MEX-CAN

Wine festivals are an efficient and fun way to experience a wide variety of wines quickly. Instead of buying bottle after bottle of wine, you may not like, you pay one price to try many wines in small amounts. In addition to tasting, you can meet winemakers, attend educational sessions, hear live music, and sample gourmet food. I list well-established festivals in or near wine-producing regions covered in this book.

California

North Coast Wine Competition

This festival offers wine lovers the opportunity to taste the North Coast AVA's best wines. The North Coast AVA wineries are from Napa, Lake, Marin, Mendocino, Solano, and Sonoma counties. The annual event is sponsored by *The Press Democrat* newspaper. The featured wines have achieved both a gold medal and at least a 90-plus point rating in The Press Democrat's wine competition.

Sonoma Wine Country Weekend

Every September in Sonoma County, the local wine auction grants visitors the opportunity to taste wine made by local winemakers. While the auction is the main event, the weekend is filled with lunches and dinners hosted at various Sonoma vineyards.

Paso Robles Wine Festival

Held every May, and presents a wide range of regional wines. The whole town turns out for the festival, complete with live music.

San Diego Bay Wine Festival

Under the sunny skies of southern California, held every November, is the San Diego Bay Festival, the biggest in south California. Renowned winemakers and America's top culinary talent come to the festival to offer a unique wine and food experience.

Monterey Wine Festival

The Monterey Wine Festival has been held for over forty years. It is the premier wine and food event in Monterey. The event runs for a full weekend in June, featuring food paired with beers, spirits, and world-class wines. The festival includes a cocktail camp, an array of craft spirits, plus craft beer, and music.

Washington State

Taste Washington

This is a four-day festival in Seattle that attracts thousands of wine lovers and has been held for over twenty years. The annual event is billed as their largest single-region wine and food event. It ranks among USA Today's 10-Best Wine Festivals. Recently, the event recruited 240 Washington wineries and 70 Pacific Northwest restaurants.

Catch the Crush

An annual harvest and wine festival celebrated in mid-October in the Yakima Valley region, two hours from Seattle. The event includes grape stomping, live music, culinary events, and excellent local wine.

Oregon

Spring Barrel Wine Tasting Event

Yakima Valley wine tasting from the barrel is a unique experience held annually in April. Expect wines to taste different than out of the bottle since the vintages are brand new, giving tasters a sneak peek into how they mature. You have two weekends to participate, and many wineries are open for pre-barrel tastings.

International Pinot Noir Celebration

The three-day event is famous worldwide as a mecca for Pinot Noir and northwest cuisine lovers. During the weekend, world-renowned wine-makers, northwest chefs, esteemed media, epicures, and wine lovers will gather in McMinnville, Oregon, for exploring Pinot Noir, savoring unforgettable meals, while learning and celebrating with luminaries of the food and wine world.

Whether tasting Grand Cru Burgundy or walking through Oregon vineyards with the grower who planted them, guests find themselves unwinding in picturesque Oregon wine country for what wine legend Jancis Robinson described as one of the most enjoyable wine weekends in the world.

Northwest Food and Wine Festival

The annual Northwest Food and Wine Festival has become the traditional wine festival in Portland. The festival brings the highest quality regional wines, spirits, beers, foods, and prominent chefs and restaurants.

New York

Niagara Wine Festival

In September, the Niagara Wine Festival offers over one hundred different events while celebrating Niagara's bounty of the harvest with fresh wines and perfectly paired dishes from all over the region.

Finger Lakes Wine Festival

The Finger Lakes Wine Festival was named Best Wine Festival in the U.S. by USA Today readers. It is held each July at Watkins Glen International raceway in Watkins Glen, NY. The food and wine event fuses wine tasting with regional artisans, music, culinary classes, cooking demonstrations, and breweries and draws thousands of visitors each year. Camping, glamping, and pace car rides at Watkins Glen International raceway are also available.

Ice Wine Festival

Annually in February, this unique winter festival, hosted by Casa Larga Vineyards in Fairport NY, celebrates the sweet dessert wines produced from grapes that freeze naturally on the vine. The wine festival offers visitors ice wine samples from various New York wineries, an ice wine-infused menu, horse-drawn wagon rides through the vineyard, ice wine tours, seminars, chef cook-offs, and more.

Canada

Niagara Grape & Wine Festival

This Niagara Ice Wine Festival has been held in January for over sixty-five years with sponsored events, local winery events, and a parade.

The Okanagan Wine Festivals Spring Wine Festival

This annual festival is the first of four seasonal British Columbia wine festivals with signature events and winery-specific happenings beginning in May.

Mexico

Grape Harvest Fiestas

The Association of winemakers of Baja California, Mexico holds the annual Grape Harvest Fiestas in the Valley of Guadalupe in Ensenada, Mexico, every year in August. The celebration includes wine tastings sessions, concerts, and soirées, samplings of regional cuisine, and Mexican wines.

Virginia

Virginia Wine Expo

Lonely Planet named Richmond in its Top Ten must-visit list of the U.S. destinations you need to see. If there is one event in Richmond that encapsulates the excellent craft beverage and food scene in Virginia, it is the Virginia Wine Expo.

Taste of Monticello Wine Trail Festival

Wine Enthusiast magazine recently dubbed the Charlottesville area as one of the world's top wine destinations. With tens and tens of wineries in the beautiful Blue Ridge Mountain area, the festival celebrates and embodies the area's affinity for great wine. The wine festival includes special winemaker events and the Monticello Cup Awards celebration. It culminates with a massive wine tasting of various local wines from area wineries.

Virginia Wine Festival

In October, the forty-fifth annual Virginia Wine Festival is held at upscale One Loudoun in Ashburn, Virginia. Taste over two hundred Virginia wines, dozens of ciders, sample local cuisine, and buy wine by the bottle and case. Take them home to enjoy all year with your complimentary Virginia wine tasting glass.

SOUTHERN HEMISPHERE

South American countries have a long history of wine production, with immigrants planting vines from Spain, Italy, and France as early as the 1500s. The southern part of the continent is in the wine-producing temperate zone suitable for quality wine production. There are currently four major wine-producing countries in South America. Argentina and Chile export their wine worldwide, while Brazil and Uruguay principally produce wine for domestic and local markets.

Australia, New Zealand, and South Africa round out the list of fine wine producing countries in the Southern Hemisphere. Australia and New Zealand are known for being innovators and early adopters of wine making techniques and produce world class wine in many categories. South Africa has a long history of wine production and its wine is well positioned between New and Old Word styles.

ARGENTINA

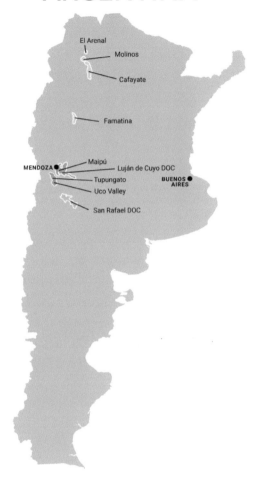

Argentina is a significant producer and exporter of wine, coming in fifth in world wine production behind France, Italy, Spain, and the U.S. The growing conditions in western Argentina near the Andes mountains are favorable for wine grapes with sunny, dry, high altitudes. Argentina makes high-quality signature wines from well-known French grapes and ancient grapes brought to Argentina by the Spanish.

Historical Tidbit - The Altura Maxima vineyard in the Molins subregion of Salta is located at 10,200-foot elevation, making it the highest vineyard in the world.

Hierarchy Of Argentinian Wine

Argentina has three tiers of wine classification modeled after the European system. I.P. (Indicacion de Procedencia) is the base level and is considered table wine. Eighty percent of I.P. wine must come from grapes in its region. I.G. (Indicacion Geografica) is a step up in quality from I.P. where wine is made from grapes grown, vinified, and bottled in a designated area. The top quality is DOC (Denominaicon de Origen Controlada), where regulations specify grape types allowed, geographic boundaries, how many grapes per plant, and more.

Notable Appellations

Mendoza is the central winegrowing region with five sub-regions. The most notable are *Tupungato* and the *Uco Valley* regions; they produce excellent, highly rated Malbec, Chardonnay, and Bordeaux blends. The *Maipu* region close to the city of Mendoza also produces excellent wine. Of note, two of Mendoza's sub-regions have obtained DOC status: *The San Rafel DOC* and the *Lujan de Cuyo DOC*.

Salta sits in the northern winegrowing region and is known for light, crisp, floral white wines. Salta has high altitude vineyards reaching above 10,000 feet elevation with three major subregions: *El Arenal, Molinos,* and well-known *Cafayate.*

Recommended Signature Wine

Try Argentina's signature white grape, Torrontes, from the *Cayfayate* region in the northern Salta area. These are light yellow colored, aromatic, perfumed wines. They have firm acidity, light-bodied, and are fresh with intense aromas of spice and flowers.

For a red recommendation, try a Malbec from the *Uco Valley* region. These are dark-colored wines with lots of body and medium acidity. The aromas are of chocolate, jam, and black fruit, such as cherries and raspberries. The tannins are medium but firm, and Malbecs tend to be on the higher side of the alcohol range.

Classification

Vinos Finos - a regulated term for wines made from premium, permitted grape types. Wine is produced from at least eighty-five percent of the grape type stated.

Reserva – these are Vinos Finos wines aged at least six months for whites and one year for reds before released for sale.

Gran Reserva – these are Vinos Finos wines aged at least one year for whites and two years for reds before released for sale.

BRAZIL

Brazil produces wine from Italian and French grapes in three states, Rio Grande do Sul, Santa Catarina, and Bahia. The state of Santa Catarina has a small wine production region at high elevations. With a tropical climate, Bahia state produces wine in small amounts in the Vale do Sao Francisco region, winning awards for their sparkling wine of late. The bulk of production is in the most southern state of Rio Grande do Sul.

Historical Tidbit

Jesuit missionaries first planted wine grapes in the state of Rio Grande do Sul for sacramental wine in the 1600s. Today the wine industry there is dominated by descendants of Italians who immigrated to Brazil in the 1800s.

Notable Appellations

Serra Gaúcha in Rio Grande do Sul produces eighty-five percent of Brazil's wine. Serra Gaúcha's sub-region, *Vale dos Vinhedos,* is currently the only region in Brazil to earn DO status, the highest level of quality in the Brazilian system. The region's focus is on red wine using Italian and French grape types of Barbera, Cabernet Sauvignon, Merlot, Cabernet Franc, Tannat, and Trebbiano. Also, Serra Gaúcha is gaining international attention with its good quality sparkling wine.

Recommended Signature Wine

Try a red wine made from *Merlot* grapes from the *Vale dos Vinhedos DO*. These are earthy wines with dried herbs, black plum, black currant, carob notes, and nutty sweetness. They are medium to full-bodied, exceptionally smooth, with bright acid and a bit of tannin on the palate.

CHILE

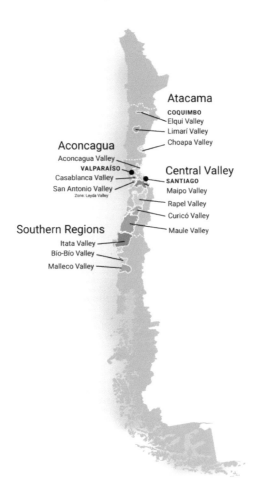

Atacama
COQUIMBO
Elqui Valley
Limarí Valley
Choapa Valley

Aconcagua
Aconcagua Valley
VALPARAÍSO
Casablanca Valley
San Antonio Valley
Zone: Leyda Valley

Central Valley
SANTIAGO
Maipo Valley
Rapel Valley
Curicó Valley
Maule Valley

Southern Regions
Itata Valley
Bío-Bío Valley
Malleco Valley

The wine region of Chile runs for hundreds of miles along the cool Pacific coast of South America. Chile's climate is somewhere between California and France, with the best wine regions protected by coastal mountains in valleys west of the towering Andes. Chile uses well-known French grapes for its wine production, making excellent wine for its large export market.

Historical Tidbit - Chile was never attacked by phylloxera, an aphid-like louse that devastated European vineyards in the 1800s.

Hierarchy Of Chilean Wine

Chile has geographic wine regions called Denominacion de Origen (DO) structured like the U.S. AVA system. There are no restrictions on grape varieties or viticultural practices, and truth-in-labeling prevails over regulations. Chilean wine will be labeled with the type of grape used and a geographic indicator. Chile uses oak aging for many of its premium wines.

Notable Appellations

Maipo Valley is close to urban Santiago, with old vines producing its best wine with Cabernet Sauvignon grapes.

Rapel Valley has two subregions, the *Cachapoal Valley* and *Colchagua Valley*. These regions produce excellent red wine from the French grapes Cabernet Sauvignon, Merlot, Syrah, and Carménère.

Recommended Signature Wine

Try a red wine made from the Cabernet Sauvignon grape from the *Colchagua Valley region*. These wines are very reasonably priced for the value. They are dark-colored wines with violets, plum, and blueberry aromas. The flavors are succulent and juicy with blueberry flavors. The acidity is medium, and tannins and alcohol tend to be high.

Another red recommendation is made with the *Carménère* grape from the *Colchagua Valley region*. These are deep red wines, with the full-bodied styles having floral notes of violet with dark fruit such as blackberries and blueberries. The tannins are not overpowering, and the acidity is balanced.

URUGUAY

Uruguay's primary wine region is in the south of the country, near the capital Montevideo. This region produces high-quality wine from its signature grape Tannat. The origin of Tannat is from the French Basque region in southwest France, where it is still grown. Uruguay makes good reds, red blends, and hearty rosés from Tannat.

Historical Tidbit

Tannat arrived in Uruguay in the 1800s from Basque country in Europe. Don Pascual Harriague, a French Basque himself, was influential in the propagation of Tannat throughout the country.

Recommended Signature Wine

Try a *Tannat* from Uruguay characterized by elegant, soft tannins and fruit notes of ripe blackberry, jam, chocolate, and spice with saline touches and medium tannins.

AUSTRALIA

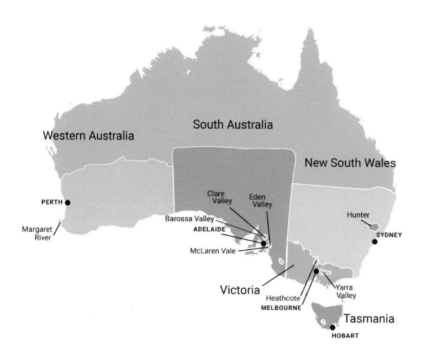

Australia is the size of the United States, but its northern tier is too hot and dry for winegrowing. The bulk of its signature wine is produced in the southeast part of the country, close to the ocean. The island of Tasmania, south of the mainland, has a growing wine industry producing signature wines from grapes that do well in cooler climates.

Historical Tidbit

According to Wikipedia, Australia is the oldest, flattest, and driest inhabited continent.

Hierarchy Of Australian Wine

Australia has a place of origin system like the U.S. AVA system. There are no restrictions on grape varieties or viticultural practices. Truth in labeling prevails over regulations, and Australian wine is labeled with the type of grape used and a geographic indicator.

Australia has created a geographical indication system (G.I.s) that defines different size regions, largest to smallest they are: Country, Multistate, State, Super Zone/Zone, Region, Subregion. The smallest winegrowing areas called subregions are defined by climate, and soil makeup, presumably producing wines with distinct characteristics.

Notable Wine Zones And Regions

South Australia Zone

Barossa Valley South Australia's prestigious winegrowing region, known for Shiraz.

McLaren Vale is a warm region, known for Shiraz.

Clare Valley is known for excellent wine from Riesling grapes.

Eden Valley known for its high-altitude vineyards producing minerally, dry Rieslings.

New South Wales Zone

Hunter Valley known for wine from the Semillon grape.

Victoria Zone

Rutherglen know for Shiraz and fortified wine from the Muscat grape.

Beechworth home to famous wineries producing excellent Chardonnay, Pinot Noir, and Shiraz.

Yarra Valley and Mornington Peninsula great Pinot Noir and Chardonnay.

Heathcote known for top-quality Shiraz.

Western Australia Zone

Margaret River known for exceptional white wine from Chardonnay and Sauvignon Blanc grapes.

Tasmania produces excellent still and sparkling wine from Pinot Noir and Chardonnay grapes.

Recommended Signature Wine

Try a white wine made from the Chardonnay grape from the *Margaret River district's Western Australia zone.* These are fresh, zippy Chardonnays with floral and citrus aromas with ripe pear, white peach flavors, medium-bodied with creamy weight, and a little spicy oak.

For a starting point with Australian red wines, try one made from Shiraz grapes from the *Barossa Valley*. These wines are full-bodied, supple, and expressive, with firm tannins, tar and tea aroma, dark fruit, and berries wrapped in pleasing spice flavors.

Classification

Best Before Date: found on some Australian wine labels and applies for wine with a shelf life of fewer than two years.

GSM: blends made famous in Australia consisting of Grenache, Shiraz (Syrah), and Mourvèdre.

SGM: blends where Shiraz is the main grape used along with Grenache and Shiraz.

Stickies: this is the name for sweet, fortified dessert wines of Australia.

NEW ZEALAND

New Zealand is a South Pacific island country belonging to the British Commonwealth, formed, and shaped by volcanic activity. Wine is produced in the maritime climate on both its main islands, North Island and South Island. It has a diverse environment affected by ocean currents, mountain ranges, lakes, rivers, and an extensive coastline. New Zealand exports more wine than it consumes and has signature wines made from French and German grape types. Producers use grape types on labels along with a geographic indicator of the origin of the wine.

Historical Tidbit

The remote islands of New Zealand are 1,200 miles east of Australia. They are the last large landmass discovered by humans in the mid-second century A.D.

Notable Wine Regions

Hawke's Bay

Hawke's Bay is located on the North Island's warm eastern side. It is New Zealand's second-largest wine producer behind Marlborough. The warm region is favorable for producing red wines from Cabernet Sauvignon, Merlot, Syrah grapes and white wines from Chardonnay, Sauvignon Blanc, and Viognier grapes. Also, Merlot blends and Syrah from this region are excellent.

Marlborough

Marlborough is located on the South Island's northern tip and is New Zealand's largest producer and wine exporter. Marlborough Sauvignon Blanc has an international reputation for its unique, delicious blend of New and Old-World flavors. Red Pinot Noir from Marlborough is praised for being consistently good with rich, deep-colored Pinot Noir and a distinct taste profile compared to the benchmark French Burgundies.

Recommended Signature Wine

Try a white wine made with Sauvignon Blanc grapes from the *Marlborough* region. These are wines with a lively aroma of grapefruit, passion fruit, apricots, peaches, nectarines, and grassy green notes. They are light-bodied wines with mouth cleansing acidity and a pleasing long finish.

For a starting point with red New Zealand wines, try one made from Pinot Noir grapes from the *Marlborough* region. These wines are of consistent quality, are silky smooth, and complex. Producers use French oak barrels resulting in soft, fragrant, and flavorful wines with aromas of ripe cherries and dark fruit.

SOUTH AFRICA

European vines were planted in South Africa in the mid sixteen hundred by the Netherlanders, aka the Dutch. The South African wine region is located on the ocean at the southern tip of the African continent, with a favorable climate and a significant port. South Africa was a wine producer for European markets from the mid sixteen hundred to the late 1800s. Today, they make excellent red, white, and sweet wine with signature French grapes and hybrids. The Pinotage grape was cultivated here in 1925, a cross between the Pinot Noir and Cinsault grapes, and it is now South Africa's signature red wine grape.

Historical Tidbit

The sweet dessert wine Vin de Constance was loved by non-other than Presidents George Washington, John Adams, and Thomas Jefferson. Authors Jane Austen and Charles Dickens, poet Baudelaire, and the Emperor of France, Napoleon Bonaparte loved this wine too!

Hierarchy Of South African Wine

South Africa has defined geographic wine regions that follow wine laws like the U.S. AVA system. There are no restrictions on grape varieties or viticultural practices. Truth in labeling prevails over regulations, and South African wine will be labeled with the type of grape used and a geographic indicator. South Africa has put a Wine of Origin Scheme in place that defines different size regions, largest to smallest: Geographical Units (G.U.), Regions, Districts, and Wards. The smallest winegrowing areas called Wards are determined by climate and soil makeup.

Notable Wine Regions

Stellenbosch an old and excellent wine district, the Pinotage grape is successfully used here.

Paarl known for intense, fruity, robust red wine and fruity, tropical white wine.

Franschhoek Valley i.e., The French Corner, known for wine from French grapes.

Constantia Ward produces Vin de Constance, a delicious, sweet wine.

Swartland know for Rhône grape types and Chenin Blanc.

Walker Bay a cool coastal area, known for Chardonnay and Pinot Noir

Recommended Signature Wine

Try a red Pinotage from the *Stellenbosch District* made from the Pinotage grape. The grape was developed in South Africa and makes a deep red wine with fruity bouquet aromas of ripe banana, toffee, cinnamon, plums, and prunes. It is a medium-bodied wine with lots of berry flavors and medium, pleasing tannins.

A must-try is the sweet dessert wine, Vin de Constance, from the *Constantia Ward*. This is a decadent, full-bodied, and dense wine, with aromas of fruit, perfume, sweet, earthy, hints of toffee, shaved wood, and honeysuckle.

Classification

Noble Late Harvest: wine made from grapes (mostly Chenin Blanc grapes)

affected by botrytis, aka noble rot.

Vin de Constance: A South African dessert wine made from Muscat Blanc à Petits Grains grapes.

Single vineyard: is a wine from a defined area of fewer than thirteen acres.

Estate Wine: is a wine from an estate controlling their vineyards and producing wine on the premises.

CHECKLIST OF
SIGNATURE WINE

This is intended for your record keeping and an aide while shopping for wine. An example of use would be to ask a wine merchant for the *California* wine section, then for *red Cabernet Sauvignon* from the *Calistoga AVA*.

California

Napa Valley AVA

☐ **Cabernet Sauvignon** - red, Calistoga AVA

☐ **Chardonnay -** white, Los Carneros AVA

Sonoma

☐ **Chardonnay** - white, Chalk Hill AVA

☐ **Zinfandel -** red, Dry Creek Valley AVA

☐ **Zinfandel -** red, Rock Pile AVA

☐ **Cabernet Sauvignon** - red, Alexander Valley AVA

San Francisco Bay AVA

☐ **Chardonnay** - white, Livermore Valley AVA

☐ **Zinfandel -** red, Santa Clara AVA

☐ **Cinsault** - red, Lodi AVA, Bechthold Vineyards, ancient vines

Sierra Foothills AVA

☐ **Syrah / Mourvèdre** - red, El Dorado AVA

Central Coast AVA

☐ **Chardonnay** - white, Monterey AVA

☐ **Zinfandel** - red, Paso Robles AVA

South Coast AVA

☐ **Cabernet Franc** - red, Temecula Valley AVA

Washington State

☐ **Cabernet Sauvignon** - red, Horse Heaven Hills AVA

☐ **Syrah** - red, Walla Walla Valley AVA

Oregon

☐ **Pinot Noir** - red, Willamette Valley AVA

New York

☐ **Cabernet Franc** - red, Seneca Lake AVA

☐ **Riesling** - white, Keuka Lake AVA

Virginia

☐ **Viognier** - white, Monticello AVA

☐ **Petit Manseng** - white, Middleburg AVA

- ☐ **Meritage** - red, Monticello AVA, blend, Bordeaux grapes

- ☐ **Norton** - red, Middleburg AVA, Norton grape

Canada

- ☐ **Ice-wine** - white, Niagara Peninsula appellation

- ☐ **Pinot Noir** - red, Okanagan Valley of British Columbia region

Mexico

- ☐ **Nebbiolo** - red, Valle de Guadalupe

Argentina

- ☐ **Torrontes** - white, Cayfayate region

- ☐ **Malbec** - red, Uco Valley region

Chile

- ☐ **Cabernet Sauvignon** - red, Colchagua Valley region

- ☐ **Carménère** - red, Colchagua Valley region

Brazil

- ☐ **Merlot** - red, Vale dos Vinhedos DO

Uruguay

- ☐ **Tannat** - red, Uruguay

Australia

- [ ] **Chardonnay** - white, Margaret River District

- [ ] **Shiraz** - red, Barossa Valley

New Zealand

- [ ] **Sauvignon Blanc** - white, Marlborough region

- [ ] **Pinot Noir** - red, Marlborough region

South Africa

- [ ] **Pinotage** - red, Stellenbosch District, Pinotage grape

- [ ] **Vin de Constance** - white sweet dessert, Vin de Constance Constantia Ward, Muscat Blanc à Petits Grains grape

GLOSSARY

Acid: Naturally occurring grape acids that taste fresh, like orange juice or a tart apple.

Aerated Sparkling Wine: A term found on wine labels for sparkling wine with injected CO_2 to create bubbles, as in carbonated soft drinks.

Aeration: Exposing wine to oxygen by swirling in a glass or pouring into another vessel.

Appellation: A defined and understood geographic area designated for producing wine.

Aroma: These are the smells unique to a grape variety.

Blanc de Blanc: White wine from white grapes.

Body/full body: How heavy or thick a wine feels in the mouth.

Botrytis: Botrytis cinerea, referred to as noble rot. A grape fungus that concentrates a grape's juice.

Bouquet: The collection of all aromas after a wine has aged in a bottle.

Brix: A measure of grape sugar at harvest.

Brut: Very dry Champagne, with no detectable sweetness.

Chewy: A description of wine that seems almost chewable, dense, or sticky.

Complex: A wine with pleasing aromas and flavors that develop as you drink.

Dark/black fruit: Aromas and flavors found in wine resembling dark-colored fruit, ex: plums, blackberries, black cherries.

Decant: Pouring wine out of the bottle and leaving the sediment behind.

Demi-sec: A semi-sweet wine.

Dry wine: A wine with no detectable sweetness, 0.2% or less sugar.

Earthy: Aroma found in wine like the smells of soil, mushrooms, leaves, the forest.

Estate bottled: Wine from an estate that does everything from growing to bottling.

Fault: A defect with wine, usually detected by bad, odd, off-putting smells and tastes.

Finish: The taste and feel of wine once swallowed. Long-lasting flavors are considered better.

Fortified wine: Wine blended with brandy and containing between sixteen and twenty percent ABV.

Hot: Wine where alcohol is detected over other flavors and aromas.

Lees: Yeast after fermentation. Sur lie is a French term meaning the wine is left in contact with yeast cells to improve its flavor and texture.

Legs: streaks of wine running down the inside of a glass, also called tears or church windows.

Meritage: since Bordeaux is a protected placename, this invented word is used for marketing Bordeaux blends. Usually, the grapes used are Cabernet Sauvignon, Merlot, and Cabernet Franc. The Meritage Association created this term, and strict regulations apply. An example regulation is a Meritage must be a winery's most expensive wine.

New World wine: A term used to express wine not from Europe and has a prominent fruitiness.

Nose: The smell of wine.

Oxidation: The reactions in a substance when oxygen combines with its molecules, as when steel rusts when exposed to air.

Pétillant: Lightly sparkling.

PetNat: an abbreviation for naturally pétillant (bubbly) wine that is slightly sweet, gently fizzy, and low alcohol.

Red fruit: Aromas and flavors found in wine resembling red-colored fruit, ex: cherries, cranberries, strawberries.

Reserve: better or best wine from a producer. This is a regulated word in some U.S. states and Europe.

Residual sugar: Grape sugar remaining after fermentation in semi-sweet, sweet wine and dessert wine.

Single varietal: Wine made with only one grape type.

Smoky: The aroma or flavor of smoke in wine occurs naturally and is caused by barrel aging.

Sulfites: Naturally occurring and added to wine to help preserve it.

Tannin: A plant compound that tastes a little bitter and can cause a drying sensation in the mouth.

Terroir: All aspects affecting wine, the climate, location, soil, and winemaking practices.

Vintage year: Wine released on a year of good production.

Vintage: wine produced from a specific year's grapes, as in a 2020 vintage.

Winegrowing: All aspects of wine production from the vineyard to the bottle.

RECOMMENDED BOOKS

These are books that I have used to study, learn and some are for enjoyment only. I took the liberty to capture what the authors themselves said about their books, in whole or part.

Certified Specialist of Wine Study Guide

by The Society of Wine Educators

This is an educational resource published by the Society of Wine Educators and intended for candidates preparing to take the Certified Specialist of Wine (CSW) Exam.

I Drink Therefore I am

by Roger Scruton

We are familiar with the medical opinion that a daily glass of wine is good for the health and the rival opinion that any more than a glass or two will set us on the road to ruin. Whether or not good for the body, Scruton argues, wine, drunk in the right frame of mind, is definitely good for the soul. And there is no better accompaniment to wine than philosophy. By thinking with wine, you can learn not only to drink in thoughts but to think in draughts. This good-humored book offers an antidote to the pretentious claptrap that is written about wine today and a profound apology for the drink on which civilization has been founded.

The Essential Guide to Wine

by Madeline Puckette and Justin Hammack

The Essential Guide to Wine will help you make sense of it all in a unique infographic wine book. Designed by the Wine Folly website's creators, which has won Wine Blogger of the Year from the International Wine & Spirits Competition, this book combines sleek, modern information design with data visualization.

The New Sotheby's Wine Encyclopedia

by Tom Stevenson

Sotheby's Wine Encyclopedia reflects the most recent trends in the dynamic world of wine, written by experts worldwide. Beautifully illustrated with more than 400 images and 100 National Geographic maps, this definitive guide is arranged geographically to highlight the regions and climates that produce the best vintages. From Southeast Europe to the Eastern Mediterranean, each page is packed with information on flavor notes, vineyard profiles, tasting room guides, grape know-how, and special information on unique varietals. The book also features top wines organized by maker and year; a troubleshooter's guide to potential wine faults; a taste chart to help identify flavors; up-and-coming producers; unusual wines, food pairings, and more.

The Oxford Companion to Wine

by Oxford Press

Combining meticulously-researched fact with refreshing opinion and wit, This work presents almost 4,000 entries on every wine-related topic imaginable, from regions and grape varieties to the owners, connoisseurs, growers, and tasters in wine through the ages. From viticulture and oenology to the history of wine, from its origins to the present day.

The Sommelier's Atlas of Taste: A Field Guide to the Great Wines of Europe

by Rajat Parr and Jordan Mackay

This book is the first definitive reference book to describe, region-by-region, how the great wines of Europe should taste. This will be the go-to guide for aspiring sommeliers, wine aficionados who want to improve their blind tasting skills, and amateur enthusiasts looking for a straightforward and visceral way to understand and describe wine.

The Wine Bible

by Karen MacNeil

Like a lively course from an expert teacher, The Wine Bible grounds the reader deeply in the fundamentals while layering on informative asides, tips, amusing anecdotes, definitions, glossaries, photos (all new for this edition), maps, labels, and recommended bottles. Karen MacNeil's information comes directly through primary research; for this second edition, she has tasted more than 10,000 wines and visited dozens of wine regions worldwide. New to the book are wines of China, Japan, Mexico, and Slovenia.

The World Atlas of Wine

by Hugh Johnson

Critics recognize it as the essential and most authoritative wine reference work available.

Understanding Wine Technology

by David Bird

Any student who has ever logged credits in a viticulture and enology class knows Bird's book. It is the most widely assigned wine science primer in the English-speaking world. Bird's classic textbook deciphers all the new scientific advances that have cropped up in the last several years and conveys them in his typically clear and plainspoken style that renders even the densest subject matter freshman friendly.

Wine: A Tasting Course: Every Class in a Glass

by Marnie Old

Demystify wine with this ultimate visual course for wine lovers. Think while you drink with Wine A Tasting Course. A fresh take on the world of wine, showing you what you need to know and exploding wine myths. Cannot smell honeysuckle or taste tobacco? So, what. Wine A Tasting Course focuses on you, helping you to discover which wines you like and why.

Wine Speak

by Bernard Klem

If you read wine reviews, you are already either amused or confused by the soaring language wine writers often use to describe what they are smelling and tasting. But do you always know what they mean? Have you ever sipped a complex white and sensed what is so colorfully described as a peacock's tail? If not, you are in for a treat because these terms and many more are all here to amuse, dismay, enlighten, inspire, puzzle, and shock you.

Printed in Great Britain
by Amazon